# CROSSROADS

# OF STOLEN TIME

# CROSSROADS OF STOLEN TIME

*A Theme of Targeted Occult Abduction and The Forfeit of Our Origins*

TITANIA WYCHWOOD

I sit down to write this story in the tech of silence... a cultural commentary, a character study, a glimpse of the cult of group mind control, and stealth from humanity and its amnesiac condition.

# TABLE OF CONTENTS

# CHAPTER 1
## *Mother Wound and The Fallen*

There was a disconnect.

If I were to trace where it really started, I would say the womb.

It appeared to be one of these accidental arrangements, where compatibility, or what is referred to as natural selection, was cranky.

A panicked instinct was formed instead.

I did not bond with my mother as human infants do best. An inheritance of ancestral and past life trauma and wounding would echo chamber my destiny.

I would meet many people, who triggered an echo of that **PANICKED** instinct.

My sense of security was challenged by the worth of my experiences... Perhaps I just didn't have the chops to be loved.

A hard-wired nervous system, and those highs of drama became **THE FAMILIAR.**

We are born here, forgetting where we came from and why.

It remains one of the holographic tantalizers of our existence.

It asks for a filling of our time, like a phantom cavity, that needs something, a hissing quotient, of painful mystery.

We are born here to form an identity, one that adheres to an obstacle course, upon arrival and residence.

Abduction by tentacles of evil predation defies all manners of time and space.

One can literally feel as though they are a casualty of a great, unfortunate segue.

The art of controlling nature, and other peoples', in order to assuage deep unconscious floatsam, is a remnant of our finagled origins... playing with forces of the planet, and beyond; the dark, the deathly register of ancient power battles.

Children of a **MOTHER WOUND** signal insecurity and self-doubt.

Are they good enough? Perhaps it's their fault? ...Well, of course it is, and they apologize for their existence.

Predatorial aggressors can smell the fetidness of their preferred prey; they easily target them to elicit a sense of superior address.

These predators know all too well how their target feels. Because they do too.

Cult studies show that the entrapment of belonging, resurrecting, a 'FAMILIAR' state, is participating in something bigger and better. It is a persuasion of an ultimate designation within this disordered planet.

The book of ENOCH discusses THE FALLEN ONES, Angels of the GODLY realm. They took human form, to procreate with the magnetic women of earthly design. This, in defiance of the 'jealousy', and ultimate request, of God's decree.

Monstrous Hybrids resulted from these unions, aka The Nephilim. They plundered the earth with violence and destruction.

Disfigured and demonically led, the rebellious will of this pantheon would echo for ages.

Eugenics.

The CREATORSHIP punished this realm for these accidental and spiralling transgressions.

Contributing to the remnant of irreconcilable fissure on our planet.

A denomination of: sacrifice and forgiveness vs. worship and jealousy.

# CHAPTER 2

## *Simulations and Initiations*

There are many truths to things, as there are dimensions beyond our scope of imagination.

This environment of earthly consciousness, replicates through a simulated and synthetic reproduction. It mimics the capacities, we once possessed.

Our realm, and sentience, is used to resource the will and hunger of these dissidents of authority. A battle of rulership and ultimate will. The crude imitation of our original blueprints, ensure we are bound to feed this authority, by obscuring our connection and memories to what we really are.

Middlemen confer connection to the Highest Highs and Lowest Lows, interfering with our own supernatural connection to our original 'design'. Some of these are crudely imitated through technology.

We are no longer connected to our great force as we once were; we mock those who practice magic or alternative spirituality, but ignore that religion has a smattering of similarity.

Science and industrialization become our replicating Creator.

Payper Money. The alchemy of functional transactions, the celebration of this realm.

A neutral ground for progressing, where academia, money lending, and the Continental breakfast make it a stamp of origins.

To be upstaged by others is indeed very primal. As Ernest Becker in his book Escape from Evil elucidates, 'the fear of being reduced has a life of its own'.

The more important, or seemingly less sufferable of us, threaten to humiliate those of us who do not feel as addled.

In primal-based societies, there was, and still is, the proclivity to turn to the forces of nature and attempt to control aspects of life through ritual and magic.

It was used to destroy the threat of someone else, having the seeming ability to endure life better than they.

Jealousy, envy, and the lottery of circumstance for any of us becomes a backdrop competition:

Who has the ability to survive the best, without suffering?

Or, seeming as if they do.

This place, the result of rebel temptation realized, we are all in a loop of this sequel.

Wanting or being seduced by something seemingly better, and defying aspect of the (our) **CREATORSHIP.**

A blip in time, creating crude currency of our higher energies and connections.

What is hidden from us, the unfortunate things we experience in this realm, are **INITIATIONS.**

My original contractee of great cultivated misfortune and destruction: **THUG,** I will call her, a frequent option, as were other women, outside of my relationship, with a man I will call **SCORPIO.**

He was, himself, a survivor of his own fissures of innocence.

A dark gathering of selfishness and covert destruction - lined him, and others, in both his, and my social circles.

On 12.12.22, **SCORPIO** came into my life, as if handed by the Universe.

He had ways about him that I regretfully embraced.

This attraction, a shrill echo, of my **MOTHER FATHER WOUND** in concentration.

THIS would change my world forever.

Or... perhaps the Universe... had assigned this challenge.

I did after all, find the **FAMILIAR.**

# CHAPTER 3

## *Jealousy, Magic and Cult Foundation*

**THUG** had similar acquaintances within our social circle.

**SCORPIO** relished his power, and control over others. He provoked situations, gleefully benefitting from the attention, and craftiness of his deception and intrigue.

Manipulating many of us around him.

Not many knew **THUG** was part of an elite Satanic Ritual Abuse trafficking cult, which targeted people en masse for sacrifice, currency, revenge, and entertainment.

The irony that a Satanic cult is eager for the **'In God We Trust'** currency.

**It is THIS** currency, we are forced to trade, our time, and true creative connection to the **GREATNESS** of being alive.

Within the folds of both **SCORPIO'S** and **THUG'S** social groups hid a few elites, directly establishing this kind of organization.

**SCORPIO'S** other diabolical adores, of which about 5 of them also targeting myself and others, were keen to damage people they felt had more.

People's contribution and purpose are an objective part of the planetary scheme.

Some fit, some 'misfit.'

An Individual's blessings are theirs. Herein, primal feelings of being smaller can be stoked.

How **DOES** the Universe take care of you? What is **YOURS** intrinsically?

'Fitting In' to a contrived system is not all it's cracked up to be.

If everyone had enough of what they needed, were appreciated for what they discover, they could contribute, without force or pressure, a glorious quality of existence.

Their true connection to the **SOURCE OF ALL** — direct, of individual translation, the slice of that Holy expression you become, and it expresses through you. Freely.

We are instead, swimming in a collective's shadow.

Capitalism, communism, dictatorships, all contrived to benefit an order of a select few.

Infusing these intellectual organizations as the order that will **SAVE** us, has become another distractive installation on our planet. It reinforces the very system that annihilates us.

**Cognitive Dissonance.**

To be politically astute, by what you are led to believe is true, allows you SOME conjecture of the pure purpose of organization, and power.

The North American Natives observed the greatest shadow of humanity: **IS; JEALOUSY** and **GREED.**

When someone struggles with whether their life mattered, that **THEY** mattered, and that they could conquer all that was against them, becoming a target to an organized predatory cult: the ultimate despair.

The covertness of how people handle their own base emotions and the universal shadow, varies.

Whether it is addictions, destructive behaviours, and other forms of escape—deeply frightening, and seemingly irreconcilable feelings, of being less than, create massive shame.

In a culture that prizes 'A' contest, of criteria that runs counterintuitively to the way we were created to be, people are encouraged to criticize and even dislike themselves. The rites of passage through their tragedies, sometimes cannot be corroborated.

There is always somebody with more. Yet, there is something unique about all of us, no one else has.

A painful wound of the **AGES**.

Our ability to accept ourselves and connect **HIGHLY**, within our original blueprints, has been both punished and **STOLEN**.

How is damage of this magnitude repaired?

We are fed distractions, and encouraged to lose our senses in a variety of **FILLER** within our lost origins.

**Addictions**.

As a clairvoyant and clairaudient, these abilities would prove to be invaluable. The capacity to hear, sense, and see who my perpetrators were, where they were, and what their plans were, saved my life.

Downloads would reverberate upon waking, information as to whether, or how: **SOME** law enforcement agencies were approaching this situation, with justice, clarity, and finally, some seriousness.

An overwhelm of discoveries revealed, fraternities, judges, lawyers, magistrate systems, intelligence agents, child services, insurance, tech and other companies involved.

In addition, I would come to do some detective work by accessing searches on the original family involved, discovering a litany of fraud, mass phone numbers, property purchased transnationally, and all kinds of folks entangled in this organization.

It was a business.

# CHAPTER 4
## *Family Features*

Not everyone is suited to become a mother or father, and resent the role.

Sandra Jean Le Blanc Green was a major foundation in the basement of my story.

She surrogated my mother wound, simulating a maternal influence, at my then, **FAMILIAR.**

I began to realize I could trust no one around me, with my deepest sorrows and confusions, as heartbreaking and chaotic endings echoed throughout. My contractors were systematically unravelling my life.

How it came to be that this remote, random woman had already been commissioned to destroy me **BEFORE** we connected, baffles me to this day.

However, I had come to learn that networks such as these are **very** resourceful.

Sandra had a semi-calming southern demeanour, an uptight edge, and was astute in her responses. She seemed consistent with the type of 'mothering' that is often sought at any grand juncture of chaos.

As a vulnerable person, at this quaking juncture, the effects of my moments and self-concept were shaken. I was rendered in need of regular support.

This was part of the formula of destruction wrought upon me.

Though one can be 'psychic', and many of us are, much can still be hidden from those who master the cloaks of intention.

This would, as the situation unfolded, both surprise **AND** disappoint me.

Sandra originally hailed from Abbeville, LA, where Creole culture infuses voodoo, hoodoo, the dark and natural arts, as an amalgamated part of everyday life.

Sandra had allegiance to such a deep and dark realm that it was on another level of terrifying.

Her family of origin in Louisiana were also well-versed and involved, as a collected, organized unit.

Charles Le Blanc, Sandra's brother, I would come to learn, professionally tortured and destroyed people for decades.

'Child abuse and trafficking had become a 'rich' part of their lifestyle.

The hatred for people underscored this psychopathic simulation of some kind of God complex, refracted as a Satanic Depth.

The accepted part of their culture, the predatory aspect of destroying and trafficking people, is a step further.

She deemed herself untouchable, as her energy was potent.

I will explore this as we go on.

Her alignment and inclusion of Aristocracy, were the secondary flex.

Some connected higher-ups allowed these people free rein, to exploit the forbidden in massively profitable ways.

She had married Nathaniel Green, whose family are also, an organized crime network from Louisiana, amalgamating business and religious advantages. She was willing to ride for the high and the payoff.

Steven Green, of Dominican ancestry, had "built" his lifestyle of trafficking and torturing folks as a business for many decades, himself.

Shirley Brown Green, his wife, participated and got out of his way when he took his children into this fold. He taught them how to navigate an enterprise. Ample contacts offered, to catch fish, of this sort, on their own.

**THEIR** ancestral heritage: capturing the essence of tortured **SLAVES**, for centuries, stealing spiritual energy from their victims, to strengthen their powers of plundering. Voodoo, in fact, a healing art, was used destructively.

The **LOAs** within Voodoun practice were once slaves themselves. They are called upon to abuse, instead of heal, wreaking chaos on victims.

Manuel Canales, Sandra's third life partner, a global investor, media mogul, spanning all kinds of powerful industries and resources, offered more advantages, through the tech side of surveillance, tech torture weaponry, and trafficking.

Corrupt, untouchable, and wildly wealthy cronyism.


The more I learned about Sandra, and this organized network, the more horrified I was.

In this cluster of cult members, including the art of vampiric extenuation, spirit transfers, blood magic, cemetery magic, necromancy, and energy harvesting, revived, and preserved methods of this ancient art, were followed seriously.

Within her collective of devotees, willing or by shotgun, was a man named **MIAMI**.

He was the prized treasure of the lot; his power was a formidable instrument to harm victims with a piercing, agonizing torture.

Grabbing hold of the nervous system, depleting the blood sugar, spiking hormones, and inducing a nerve-wracking panic, it was an interference and a daily experience that skyrocketed a desperate terror, daily, and nightly.

A time-stopping agony; where, if one is not resilient... relief **BY ANY MEANS** is considered.

The intention was to destroy victims, provoking victims, to destroy themselves.

I experienced this level of shrill hellish escalation for 3 years, within the 9.5 years, day and night. Unannounced.

Eventually, MIAMI defected from the group and passed from escape, illness, and elimination.

He had however, contracted my life further to other devotees, as I began to renumerate who they were publicly.

There were torture signatures, from other members, Nathaniel Green, his brothers, sisters, and colleagues, producing other horrific effects, of tortured capture, and unrelenting failure, and demise to almost all aspects of my life.

Mary Wooden Green, Sentoria Green, another media mogul in Los Angeles. Lynell Renee Green went on to work for the Chamber of Commerce for Vallejo, CA.

Her husband, Samuel Green, was one of several siblings, a devout trafficker within the 80 + members, of this family constellation.

Lynell's own family of origin, the Paynes, were also contracted to participate in the systematic destruction of contractees.


A Paris Colvin, of Macon, GA, would receive a division of $10 million to continue to contract Sandra's victims, paying the other members stipends up to $10K weekly.

Marie Suire, Karen Le Blanc Suire, Charles LeBlanc's daughter and wife of Louisiana, would send messages to mock the loss of income, with fake job offers, also meant to terrorize their victim, and absolve a karmic reverb.

Karen was an Engineer in a large firm.

I had **NEVER** met these people.

Linda Le Blanc, Lisa Foreman, Charlene Theriot, Sandra's sisters, Mary Arcenaux, Jenlil Falgout, Cathy Domingue Landry—family to the Governor of New Orleans, Jeanette Delcambre, folks ensconced in their respective towns for generations, would continue to foster these activities, even after Sandra's demise.

Sandra even tried to tether herself to me, even after her passing, to ensure that she could still manipulate the course of my life and my spiritual connection.

Contractees in Lebanon, India, and Jamaica were other avenues of farmed ritual.

Also involved were a fraternity of Luciferians, who abused, sacrificed, and trafficked children.

Several judges in GA were invested, certain police officers, a David Simmons of the GA bar, David Cohen, George Dremel... all part of a certain order.

Emyce and Gerald Derringe, Jeremy Childs, Bryden Bryce, Sandra Lee Thomas, Terrigen, Omagen, Mary Ann, James and Pete Frazier, Linda Morales Frazier— The Stepper Community of Chicago, IL, and Atlanta, GA had many members involved.

There were notable members of the Toronto, Canada, Occult community who also contracted to target victims for years.

Jerry Paulukin of Calgary Alberta Canada, a businessman and investor, also heavily involved in these activities.

Professor Andrew Weiss, of Weiss Assets Management, Boston, and Boston U.

Dr. Martin Weiss of The Classy Investors.

Lawyer David Brennan of Smyrna, GA, his family, and brother Richard Brennan of Psytech Digital Ltd, and 7th Sense Psychics.

George Dremel, had been involved in fraternities, of which were appropriately acronymized, as KOC.

A strong German influence appeared in this Satanic organization. There are at least six located in Frankfurt and elsewhere in Germany, who oversee stalking, torture, and harassment of victims.

A powerful German Jewish judge oversaw these operations at a very high level.

A voyeuristic genocide.

A prominent judge in Germany, uses GA as a money laundering threshold, to an insurance company. Insurance policies against victims, drives the relentless abuse. A closed Magistrate system in GA, seems to protect the most High.

David Miller and his wife Joan of Carlsbad CA, involved in insurance fraud, policies against their victims, a bait for the relentless abuse.

Law enforcement in Mississippi, billionaires in France, Holland were part of the operations as well.

Many police bribed, and part of it.

The Nevada Attorney General's office replied, it was not part of their jurisdiction while many members were in Paradise Nevada and Las Vegas.

Displaced US citizens, immigrants, and locals, are offered privileges of 'membership'.

Folks from Jamaica, especially in military or diplomatic status, were involved.

I got called by wives and children of these members, as a seeming random form of harassment.

I will mention more below.

African, Congolese, Cameroonians...it was as if some aspect of apartheid had become alchemized, for an even uglier cause.

Willing Mexican natives, also employed for their spiritual practices.

At least there is no racism in this 'model'.

The admiration for the inborn spiritual power these cultures possessed, was utilized to gain even more power, for darker purposes.

The magistrate system in Georgia, USA, where a confluence of trafficking, corrupt child services, and a bribery system operates, enables these types of activities to flourish.

The magistrate system appears to be complicit and oath-bound to this system of sealed power.

Within the folds of this network, blood oaths created, immigrants or enslaved humans are told: do our bidding of ritual torture and harassment, or die.

These contractors are monitored, even if higher ups are in prison.

It is life and death all around.

Sandra's clients, like other high-ranking officials, were on the West Coast of the US.

**The 'You Knighted States'.**

**'IN CHANCE WE TRUST'.**

Las Vegas Nevada, caters to a very hedonistic amusement park shuffle and has a high incidence of supply and demand; they, of course, must kneel for reasons that, if one understands, must be precipitated.

Hundreds of reports were ignored.

Even when folks refer to the term 'Gang Stalking', the victims are described as a group of people who are basically delusional.

**I DID NOT** use this term.

This is the control of the World Wide Web, and the extreme censorship across the world.

Emmanuel Paul of Zoom Haiti TV and the CTN network in Largo, Florida, USA.

China was also a trafficking hub for the LeBlancs in Abbeville, LA, and the network.

These folks are situated everywhere and have purchased properties in key states, where their operations were able to run smoothly.

The theft from victims includes the strength and quality of their bloodline.

And, their souls.

The 'holy' Luciferian quest.

It is the harvesting of the reactive torture and demise of their victims, the spirit of benefit, sourced by these networks.

They would dumb down my ability to think expansively and clearly, cramp my body whilst driving, cripple my legs, my back literally sucked of energy, create shoulder pain, spine pain, shackle my ankles, block my feminine energy, torture my organs, pinch my fingers and toes, mar external attraction, block and darken the heart, create an anxiousness, and irritable state, one can barely shake.

These people monitor their work and utterly delight in their victim's tormented and helpless state.

Their victims' suffering IS their nourishment.

If their victim capitulated, they were rewarded for such a sacrifice.

There are many designs of people on the planet. Some are hardwired to be super achievers. Pumping out accomplishments and experiences, one after another, and if they didn't—they might combust, or spiral.

Others might have the designation to manage others, or another has a unique energy level, where they produce or assign less, but apply something specialized.

Others, extroversion, introversion, cerebral, artistic, musical, scientific, analytical, mechanical, behavioural, forensic, psychic...

Some of our archived origins point to classes of people.

The warrior class, the agricultural class, and the merchant class.

It goes beyond this.

Our survival is ordered by external hierarchical and fiscal insistence.

There are **RULES.**

And **RULERS.**

In groups, there are hierarchies and allegiances that linger quietly. Some are gifted well, within this framework; others are baffled by it.

People fall into certain categories, the awareness that people can be fickle and inconsistent, is a blessing.

The amnesia of humanity renders us unconscious.

Trusting others becomes a warehouse adventure, a daring revelation, and, randomly, disappointing.

We can come to trust people who do not have our best interests at heart, or who we would never suspect as such.

Through either paradigm, there is a slumber.

Sandra, this malignant design, would seek out people who may have had something she wanted, would try to steal it, and ruin their lives—relentlessly.

I had come to learn that Sandra and MIAMI were charged with child abuse in 2021-2022.

She, posing as a life coach, would prey on her clients, access their profiles, surveil all their online information, and begin to covertly derail their lives, with her associates and family.

None of them would know until it was too late.

She would collect photographs, find any personal information, and pass it around to family, associates, and anyone willing to be paid, or in debt to her, for targeting her chosen one.

Sandra was driven to control and revenge those she could not control as a child, seeking ultimate power by annihilating the trust of people, enacting the former version of her own experience.

I had come to learn, Sandra had been repeatedly raped as a child, by the men in her family.

Her sisters in Abbeville, LA, —the whole of the Green family—this legendary cult who were all corralled into having to enact an ancestral allegiance of destruction in the most powerful, relentless, and, ultimately, possessed manner.

None of them could stop if **THEIR** life depended on it.

What sadly occurs is that these practices become addictive.

They cause brain and soul damage. These parts are offered to the deities and rituals. They lose chunks of themselves. Resultantly, the 'High' becomes addictive, and to function 'properly' becomes the bigger issue.

Why would one stop?

A petty heart tends to underscore many who practice under the auspices of destroying people to offset their own misery, and resent those who have something they believe they do not.

This is where it gets emergent for their victims.

And Sandra made sure these folks were possessed to do her evil, widespread bidding.

Some of these families expected all their members to capitulate to these activities, or they would be ousted, especially as children,

These become non-negotiable blood oaths.

She trafficked some of her clients. She would destroy anything they might be looking forward to, whether it be love, career, a child, or anything that would improve or bring joy to their life path.

She would sicken her clients' babies and participate in snuff. A cacophony of folks blackmailed, manipulated, and worked on to do her bidding.

She would threaten the folks contracted within this network—they were all terrified of her.

She participated in snuff rituals.

**SACRIFICE.**

Their network went deep and wide, with installations of certain officials, who would sprout protection and leniency in any criminal findings.

Sandra was likewise addicted to adrenochrome and sedatives.

# CHAPTER 5
## *Inside the Cult*

I had countless near death experiences.

Many do not survive this designation.

By late 2020, I had come to realize something was very off in my relationship with Sandra. Sandra's covertness was getting sloppy.

It wasn't until January 3, 2021, that I shut down my contact with her as a client. Things **REALLY** began to unravel—to a next-level nightmare.

My phone and electronics would distort. My sense of perception, my environment, and communications, static and scrambled.

As magic and intent are electromagnetic, this conduit was often utilized to access where someone lives, stays, via devices.

She had such a powerful capture of accessing your personal sphere, whatever she embodied was, as **SHE** deemed it, **UNSTOPPABLE.**

A hateful revenge of the ages ensued, and I was trapped in a multilayered, practice and web of deep, dark predilections and strategies.

I had never met Sandra in person, though she may have been in my sphere, and somewhere, whilst in Los Angeles, they had detected my locations, and accessed my DNA, namely, clothing, and hair.

I had noticed items missing from my stay in Mt. Shasta in 2018; several pairs of underwear vanished from my bungalow.

I doubt it was the lexicon of beings one can definitely sense, an undeniable awareness, of star system beings, and consciousness, as this location is well observed for.

I had met several locals, who had said the things they had seen and experienced, living there; they never thought possible.

It is said there is an entry to the inner earth, where these beings, in the 6th dimension of the visual spectrum, now reside and hide.

The Greens, **MOST** of them; over 80 of them, originating from Shreveport, LA, and the Dominican Republic.

Sandra and her husband Nathaniel; their main locations were on the west coast of the US, California, and Nevada.

They invested in a horse stable, employing various jockeys, especially from South America, competing in horse racing around 2006.

They also trafficked humans through this 'cover'.

She had confessed that she would tinker with the jockeys' lives for amusement.

They both amassed wealth and clout within the western board of the US and wherever they did business.

They owned properties in North and South Carolina, Georgia, Tennessee, Florida, Louisiana, Texas, New York, Chicago, and more.

Sandra trafficked people from China, with a contact, and someone she also impersonated, named Ellen FU.

This was linked to her family in Abbeville, LA, as many in the town knew.

After filing several reports, the family constellation, scattered within law enforcement, the court system, and the media, protected the truth.

However, law enforcement in Louisiana DID eventually investigate, mitigating a thorough justice, to their findings.

Supply and demand gave this network, access to immunity from some of their clients, fellow Satanic officials.

The family was well organized, and a few of them had an ounce of conscience, where these matters were concerned.

Many of them brilliantly devised a system of owning businesses, accessing technology, and knowledge to surveil, stalk, and harass people without a seeming trace.

RichHouse Reviews, 105.5 live mobile radio, SearchMME, MME Enterprises LLC, Bizzvisual LLC, 7th Sense Psychics, just to name a few.

Despite all of her considerable wealth, it was never enough for Sandra or the others.

It was alleged she was pulling in $7 million a week from her businesses.

This is obviously **BIG** amounts of **'IN GOD WE TRUST'**, with almost as much power.

Members of this cult took turns bombarding their victims with psychological coercion, sending a barrage of fake texts, ads, emails, and profile messages about how they were able to discern anything one did, and flaunting it to the victims, attempting to cultivate panic, fear, and helplessness.

They would often do this before a voodoo or dark attack. This method of contact would ensure karma did not return to them, as the rule is, let your victims know their intentions.

Some of these emails and messages were charged with energy, messages opened, calls answered, which would permit entry of etheric assignment.

So sophisticated was this operation; terrorizing their victims, inexplicable things done, felt, and executed, were truly on a scale of credulous.

I would often get fake texts asking me if I was interested in part-time or full-time work from non-existent agencies.

This was to inform the target that their financial situation was targeted.

The amount of interference to one's life, day and night, greatly distracted one from being able to focus well, sleep, execute necessary life management, or trust anything.

Things would suddenly go missing, car trunks opening spontaneously, strange adversity out of nowhere, money lost, and this was one of their biggest features, making sure you lose money, eventually - everything.

The aim was to get their victims institutionalized, sick, disabled, or to eliminate themselves.

The use of familiars—spirits, rather monitoring spirits, following and observing you. Spyware, drones, and other advanced technologies, which are again not regulated within the spyware tech marketplaces; anyone has access to such measures, and many across various platforms abuse it.

More extensive members, owned music companies, in law societies, politics, radio shows, marketing agencies, one of them involved in snuff films, others in cartel, sideline hustles of gambling and betting, courier franchises, amalgamating industries, another; telephone directory listings, to use as a means to harass people; studying the local service providers, and pretending to issue fines, and fake notices.

While having conversations on the phone, they would send messages from VoIP numbers and paraphrase who they were speaking with.

Other members in Chicago were heavily involved in dance communities, The Steppers; many of these people were paid, contracted, and involved with victims they didn't even know, but for cash, an estimated $10,000,00 per week, was a tantalizing amount to continuously harm victims with evil intent.

Seeming associations allegedly set up for helping downtrodden women and children were, in fact, fronts for grooming the most vulnerable, as they are the most desired, for the purposes of trafficking, breeding pregnancies, adenochrome production, and Satanic Ritual Abuse.

There were other crime family connections.

Some of Manuel's contacts were involved with Caribbean broadcast and NGOs, and media projects; his reach was staggering.

My reports rolled out during the pandemic, which meant very little was going to be addressed around them, then.

I did not know the scope of players yet.

I have, to date, in this late Fall of 2025, reported at least 300 times with full disclosure of proof, names, faces, etc.

In 9 years, there were over 700 people who were personally involved in my destruction.

About $6 million invested.

I screen shot evidence, death threats, fake calls, all designed to orchestrate a program of reaching their victim to enlist their energy, and then they would hone in on it, and begin to elicit whatever they wanted.

Your attention was theirs to steal by virtue of their signalling and contact.

A barrage of sensations designed to distract you, unbalance you, confuse you, emotionalize you, or deaden you with either numbness, anger, apathy, or depression would result.

The quintessential superstitions would arrive—black cats crossing my path, spiders, and more, that would tip me off to impending misfortune.

The dread so installed; it became a vigilant curiosity as to how it would roll out.

I had so many bounds and rituals of damage, I was a tightly wound-up ball, that could literally feel the strings in her auric field, tying up her movements, blocking her Hara line chakras. Numbing her sexual sensations and a sense of groundedness to earth and spirit were deeply tampered with.

All designed to ensure I could not access my feminine creative, spiritual heirship, or connection to the Most High.

The determination by these people to absolutely ruin me painfully and devastatingly fed their hunger; my horror, shock, and helplessness.

Hormones finagled, chronic manipulated pains, cultivated hot flashes, A whole formula of torture repeating itself—a sequence of chronic sensational intentions, systems, of body, mind, and spirit.

Not a lot was being done about my reports, and I certainly couldn't reveal the aspect of voodoo involved, even though many of these trafficking and Satanic ritual situations were usually accompanied by SRA, aka Satanic Ritual Abuse.

I was being tortured day and night, around the clock, in the most monstrous and terrifying ways.

No one was able to truly help me.

And many did not want to. They cited my desperation to get help and expose this sophisticated, organized torment as foolish, crazy, and MY fault.

There were so many of them alternating and participating.

I hid my situation; patiently and often desperately, waiting, and praying, for it to end, without having to tell many folks.

Unbelievable to many, and there is a reason why it is unbelievable.

The ability to destiny swap and steal someone's good fortune for themselves is another strategy of their 'arts'.

While our stay here is temporary, we are eternal beings, and well, allegedly, there is a balance for intentions.

I could feel a perimeter of my auric field absolutely filled in with the darkest of etheric conjure, encapsulating me in the most shadowy saturation.

Sandra would appear in the astral field and bully victims and those helping them. Shocked, and realizing just how horrific she/this, really was.

They would hear everything and change it –including prison, authorities, court, or the ending of this situation, and how.

They knew **EVERYTHING,** and manipulated it as a group effort.

They spent their abilities trying to get anyone in their group, in prison, out.

Every move was watched either astrally, or digitally.

They would consult other spiritualists, or oracles, to confirm as well.

They had adopted Lauren Green, and as with many other Satanic families, absorbed and groomed her to be a part of this 'program'.

Sandra also had a son, B, whom she had birthed from her first marriage. Visibly damaged, he had revealed the terror he had of his own mother.

Cult member children are not spared from the startling practice that they inflict on anyone else unfortunate, to their capture.

She was astutely relentless and able to operate in various realms thanks to her addled accompaniments and initiations through the demonic pantheon.

They would take turns, as this 'work' is very draining"

The group effort and the alternation of supply were essential to their success.

She was no longer human.

They would surveil near dead associates, family etc.

She stole energy from those around her—victims, family, associates, tasty morsels of breath baiting.

The hoovering of an electromagnetic vacuum would suddenly descend, at any time of the day... and suddenly a panic; my life force sucked out of me, with a jet propulsive action.

The way the voodoo and other practices were intended acted as a means of hooking and cording systems and energy, stemming the flow of divine connection, feminine and sexual energy, siphoned with such debilitating intensity.

Who else on the planet was experiencing this?... I felt alone.

Some of these members, looked themselves, resurrected.

In Haitian voodoo, it is well known that they are able to resurrect those who have been buried dead.

The scientific and mystical community, of **ANY** certain order, of folks, do get bored, want a challenge, or are hollowed remnants of orthodox funding, not in a nepotistic position, or in fact, they are.

A certain level of bygone metaphysics is preserved by families, tribes, cultures, students, masters, and designs.

The ancestral line is revered in many magical and religious communities, whether it is yours or the pantheon they provide you.

Your family line can become a legion of soul stealers, a reverb from the echo chamber; over all the missing pieces, of our amnesia.

It could be a balance righting itself, due to social, definitely spiritual, or political conditions; the underlying measure of the lawful regard, is whether it is right or wrong.

And in that concept, it becomes a wide margin of justifications, possibly seen as activism, for why one may enslave innocent people spiritually, on the backs of their ancestors, and the deities who delivered them.

The trouble with folks who do all too many rituals, especially against innocent people, or use them as emotional regulation, or petty revenge, is that they very, very often lose their sanity.

Or become very, very sick.

Karma GPSes them eventually.

They become addicted to the high of soul possession, and the effects of what they are doing to their victim (s)... ultimately everyone wants to be, or express something of merit; satisfied by **HOW** well they survive, those primitive feelings of envy and jealousy do not succumb, the feeling of being reduced or diminished.

One may be worse than the other.

The ones who seeded you here could have just one element of the original family blueprint and somehow been corrupted or damaged by the events of Earth and our evolution, or, rather, de-evolution.

# CHAPTER 6
## *Children and Ritual*

All that we can access, or do, may in fact be **FILLER,** in this simulated reality of whirled we encounter.

Whether one likes being here or not, distracting ourselves **meaningfully** is one of the panaceas to a frequently distorted condition.

Coming here, to experience our specie-al blueprint, remastered from ultra natural origins, spies; the hidden folds of this mystery.

Who deems us to express our divine time in such rote and regulated stewardship?

Why would we not be free to spend our 'time' upon this planetary realm as we wish?

Would everyone be so much happier and more fulfilled?

The possibility to access **AND** metabolize, the **FULL** potential of our minds; the frequency transmitting a rapid transformation, of form. A temporary physical conduit, in time—a construct, and space -utterly infinite.

What, I wondered, of my experience of this reality; What exactly **WAS** this place?

Why was, and is there so much predatory evil amongst the citizens of the planet?

People behave and handle the primeval in either thoughtful or destructive ways.

I will say this again: The art of controlling nature, and other people's, in order to assuage this deep unconscious floatsam, is a remnant of our finagled origins... playing with forces of the planet, and beyond, the dark, the deathly register of ancient power battles.

The human organs have a map of generative resonance to conditions.

To target certain feelings and states, the coordination in witchcraft goes as follows: **THE SPLEEN** corresponds with worry or anxiety, **THE LUNGS** and **LARGE INTESTINE** sadness, grief, and elimination. **THE KIDNEYS**, fear. **THE HEART,** cruelty, impatience, and hastiness. **THE GALLBLADDER AND LIVER,** rage and anger. **THE THYMUS, THE THYROID, THE OVARIES, THE GENITILIA,** your nervous system regulation, body temperature, and endocrine system.

With these practices, one can be rendered infertile, ill, women lose their periods, and both sexes lose their sexual sensations, drive, and so much more.

Sicknesses brought on, mental disturbances, and breakdowns.

Other methods are laser weaponry, utilizing satellite locations, or drones and microwave technology. Synthetic thoughts implanted, emotional manipulations, deep bone pain, circulatory system, muscle inflections, spinal weakening, endocrine manipulation, brain haemorrhages as well as heart palpitations.

Skin, air, body weight... and more.

How could this generate within a sophisticated society... that organized cult members, companies, associates and more, could abduct your life with a pursuant end, to destroy you systematically? Watched and hunted like an animal... psychologically manipulated, physically tortured by either tech or the dark arts, by a host of evil, determined parasites?

There is a stamp of Luciferian and Satanic reverence within these rings. Some are Voodouns, Santerians, Obeah practitioners abusing their craft. Other denominations that practice control over others, and events, secret fellowships, societies, and predilections* are numerous.

Now, within this vanguard of descript, unusual and more generally expressed features such as Satanic Ritual Abuse cults, the sacrifice of babies, humans, animals, paedophiliac tendencies, the darker inclusions of drinking blood, adenochrome consumption and production, snuff, eating human flesh... do in fact fall into this category of membership.

Pardon the pun.

Hollywood has been absorbed by this kind of ritual fellowship.

One does not gain access to mainstream entertainment without having to surrender to its directors.

After all, they **ARE**, and become, instruments of this particular order.

There are an increasing number of such cults and assignments, funded and littered across the planet. The feeding of select sentient energies, the intention of destroying them (as sacrifice), and safety.

The war behind this is the point. I will cover this.


The trafficking of children and humans, an underground, yet terrestrial, normalization, is part of this harvest of sentience, and the release of chemical, phenomenal nutrients.

This movement, if you will, is a form of **RESOURCE.**

## THE POWER OF TORTURE.

Paedophiles are drawn to the age at which they themselves were violated, and often cannot change this traumatic impression.

A chemical reaction is released from a child who is violated, and here, too, is nourishment.

I will go into this further on.

Sex, itself is a sacred. It also functions, as a battery charge.

The electromagnetic cellular spiritual creative sensational experience, its release of the unconscious into awareness, the plasma, the fluid holy waters of genesis.

An enlivening reset, for both, many, or just one, in the experience.

There are **HUMILIATION and BETRAYAL** rituals, woven into the experience of victims sustaining these kinds of abuses.

Eventually, situations will arise where some level of betrayal or reputational issue will explode, with a pervasive exposure or implausibility to it.

It ripples a mass energy that heightens trauma or group negativity, as a form of nourishment, to the ritualizers.

It could happen anywhere, and depending on the organizational efforts, can range from unfair situations that are scripted and arranged.

Many folks who are chosen as targets defy some subtle line of control, truth, or behaviour, to a chosen 'body'.

They may have angered someone in authority, the military, connected family, law enforcement, and more.

It can be jealousy... revenge...whistleblowing, the list and the arrangements are varied.

# CHAPTER 7
## *What is a Cult?*

Not everyone will follow the canon of culture(s).

There are those who thrive on upsetting the order of people and things; moreover, that IS their purposeful function, no matter how base, the cause and effect elicit. This delivers a dualistic result.

As with **THE FALLEN ONES.**

As with design, it is purposeful and functional.

'The Group' attempts to synthesize the collective energy and contribution of all, no matter how humble, into the production of consciousness.

What drives or lies, within the heart or dark, of this collective mind, greatly matters.

## THE FAMILIAR.

## WHAT IS A CULT?

Folks who slide into cults, have a similar predilection, something heroes their urgency, to feel the need to commune with an ideology, charisma, and illusion that swerves their judgement, and autonomous right, unless, of course, they are born into it.

And here is offered the definition of a cult: a relatively small group of people having religious beliefs or practices, regarded by others as strange or sinister.

A network of Satan -worshipping cults, there are other belief systems worshipped through these types of clustered organized reverences.

www.cookman.edu states,

Absolute authoritarianism, without meaningful accountability. No tolerance for questions or critical inquiry. No meaningful financial disclosure regarding budget, expenses such as an independently audited financial statement.

It traces similar, familial, origins for many.

Blaming this, gets trite. It **IS** bigger than that.

'Further, the same source states, there is a priesthood which is open to any (normally male) person with the necessary commitment. Religions, therefore, seek a mass following. Cults, however, rely on secret or special knowledge, which is revealed only to initiates by the cult's founder or his/her chosen representatives. Beliefs aren't normally published.

Let's go further into the sophistication of reference.

## SECRET SOCIETIES

According to Wikipedia, A secret society is an organization about which the activities, the events, inner functioning, or membership are concealed.

The society may or may not attempt to conceal its existence. The term usually excludes covert groups such as intelligence agencies or guerrilla warfare insurgencies that hide their activities and memberships, but maintain a public presence.

Many secret societies adhere to some form of ancient text preserved in reference to magic and knowledge, reserved for an initiated few.

Secret Societies are, more often than not, by choice and privilege.

Many function like a cult.

The shadow side of world history points to its lost civilizations, knowledge, practices, and eras, swept under the tide, a great flood, or fire.

A worthy, initiated ritualistic entrance into an alternative 'universe' of reality underscores benefits and, of course, inclusion.

Much like many social groups.

Those whom they deem as 'worthy', safe, or a benefit have a many-sided cluster.

## THE FAMILIAR.

Fraternal, religious, social, universalizing, and political ordinances.

Friedrich Nietzsche speaks of our will to power as a driving force behind all life and the basis of all moral systems.

He also believed that the exemplary human being should craft their own identity through self-realization, without relying on anything transcending that life.

This last encouragement can appear ideal.

This appears to be more of a threat to an ever monitored, discerned and synthetically imbued, transhumanism.

Sometimes, the people who do the most damage to us are covert and hide their true nature from us.

# CHAPTER 8

## *The Heretic and The Persecuted*

An anxiety would overtake me, suddenly, gnawing at my very core—so amplified and gloomy in its volume... a daunting spiral—it was intensive evil, shrouding me...

This kind of clatter had roots elsewhere, in time, for it not to be of such credulous assault and complexity.

The **HERETIC,** and the **PERSECUTED**, follow the original spiritual battle, scarcely veiled, in this time and space.

The power of **TORTURE**. The archetype of the **HERETIC. THE PERSECUTED.**

We are all actually considered as such.

This is why this realm is so controlled.

It is no accident that war establishes mass pain and suffering as a sacrifice for the ever-gnawing need for this type of nourishment.

Prisoners of war become an elevated source; the frequency of suffering extracted in a warehouse fashion.

Up to this point, I had been enduring their assaults on my existence for 9 years, **EVERY DAY, in varying intensity, day** and night.

The collection of DNA, photos, birthdate details, and access your involvements **EVERYWHERE.**

Photos of you as a child, outside of your **DNA,** are most dangerous.

My root chakra would burn, my fingers and toes pinched, bones in my shin would throb, neck vertebrae pinched, entities installed to produce reactions, or a dead spirit installed, to elicit a certain condition.

My stomach sick, the production of headaches, of laser technology targeting my hypothalamus. The attempts at inducing strokes, heart attacks, constipation, block and darken the heart chakra, my sexual sensations, etheric stakes pushed up my feet, stemming any feminine, or masculine power, cement blocks on your feet.

My bones tortured with deep bone pain, the back of my neck, spine, and shoulders are bound painfully, my hands are numbed, and my left foot is numbed out to block feminine and procreative flow.

Hip pain, back pain, headaches, knees, and upper thighs were targeted, so that when I walked, I would have to limp in pain.

Nerve pain in my neck, travelling down to my wrists, sinus and sickness caused, hearing affected by tech amplification, and inflammation.

Breasts, ovaries, spleen, sacred portal, adrenals, thyroid, thymus, lymph nodes blocked... the list goes on.

It is meant to unease your personal power/energy flow, to reduce you to your traumas, and spiral you out, into unrelenting insanity.

My finances and ability to live a regulated life were affected.

They would illicit rituals to break things I cherished, and to cause me to lose money as often as possible, by their attempts... This horror was very inclusive.

Stalking everything they could, having access to my digitals. Crafting alerts, letting me know, they were able to do it, AND get away with it.

Practitioners, I reached out to for help, could not go up against them. Or exploited me.

They, too, could be bombarded, interfered with, and stalked.

Some of them balked at my situation.

Or their egos were out of joint, because they affected little of what they could promise.

Some of them were commissioned to go against me, after the fact.

After getting substantial clearings from this heavy dross, from chosen practitioners, this group would double down their efforts to re-trap me.

IF you are **EVER** a victim of intensive witchcraft, voodoo, etc., by several members, it is hard to maintain your personal will.

This phenomenon isn't quite mainstream, and it's masterfully difficult to get away from.

But not impossible.

A necessary industry exists because of it.

A knowledge reserved for those initiated, captivated, seasoned, ancestral, or simply 'remembered.'

Ancient formulas thirsty for immortality, through plasmic, vs. alchemical approaches, required a whole different **DESIGN** of regeneration.

There were the smells. The smell of swamp, sewers, and bayous, would float and disperse in stages of the attacks. They would arrive suspiciously in my home, my car, or other places I had stayed.

Popping frequencies in my ear, created by the whispers of intent, in my case, fear, failure, and control by their intentions, and the spirits or demons conjured to deliver the commands.

Folks around me would also be manipulated, and seemed to exhibit unusual behaviour.

Too often to count, I had experienced heartbreaking reversals in the continuity of my relations.

I had almost become numb to it and eventually impervious.

Voodoo mambos, Wiccans, shamans, energy clearers, demon conjurors, spell crafters, prayer circles, faith healers, priests, deliverance pastors, psychics, spiritualists, wizards, witches, warlocks, all had easy answers; few understood the magnitude of what I was dealing with.

Some would insist it was my fault, my shortcoming, my flaw, and mine alone... I should know how to block them.

Others could not believe that someone like Sandra was capable of it, and absolutely gaslit me, because they were deemed authorities worldwide on these matters.

Sandra, and the 'Family Business' as they referred to it, also owned a church in Las Vegas, Nevada, the name, The Church of South Las Vegas, where they performed rituals in the basement, and held trafficked beings' captive.

Snuff, child porn, and coerced pregnancy were performed.

This ensured another stream of 'income'.

There were lapses, I thought it was finally over... a cruel ruse, the return more stringent; devastating in continuity.

A rage / fear mix would descend upon my psyche, my aura, my body.

Some of the members were more psychopathically disposed to hatred of women and tortured their victims as such. The rest, how much energy they could block and steal, and how much damage and destruction they could do to your immediate life.

A cocktail of doom and gloom would darken my steps; stop all pulses of beauty and tempo of life; a stretch of unending shifts, and moments.

Frequent panic, precious life stolen from me.

Even after initial charges and investigations, even prison time, they would come right back to do this activity.

Some of it was addiction, and some of it was a source of financial opportunity, and as I said, blood oaths.

Perhaps their bloodline, their conditioning of evil, or unhealed **MOTHER, FATHER, SIBLING, ANCESTRAL, CULTURAL, GENDER, RELIGIOUS, SEXUAL, COERCED, OR POVERTY CONSCIOUSNESS WOUNDS** were being corroborated.

Power over others, covert destruction, competition, and primal punishment were huddled in **THEIR** system.

**BY** design, or choice.

They wanted blood and a sadistically orchestrated triumph.

The mighty spiritual battle.

Control over the material world and the mystery of amnesia.

Rattles of a former **EPOCH.**

This reach of predatory insinuation is found in industries that help and purport to be confidential and clean in their intentions.

As with access to victims in other professional designations, this, too, possesses another frontier of predatory salaciousness.

Not everyone is involved, but there is organization within the organization.

This is why it is a phenomenon that requires vigilance.

The spiritual world, practitioners, psychics, and the like, can and do abuse, falsify, and defraud their clients.

I was horrified to discover, in essence, I had handed over an insider's tip to a very malignant example, who would most elaborately plot to destroy me.

The city I am from exhibits a frequent dark, unkind social energy signature. Though one can get along fairly, a level of opportunism, betrayal, and extreme cruelty lingers, and seems rather implanted.

There is a guilt, perhaps, unable to reconcile; stolen land, on the heels of persecution, and thief in the night arrival. It guards, its hard-won position of defense, and survival.

Unconsciously, it appears success within some of its communities, is... begrudged.

There is remnant trauma in every civilization distinct to its echo chamber of survivalism and tribalism.

Folks who may be disordered are simple, but complex about solving their own wounds and tectonic deliveries, and yet: somehow, this shrills **THEIR 'FAMILIAR'.**

They seek revenge and destruction as an art, if not a sport. They return to old traumas, to enact those feelings, trying to control them, by experiencing them, in current situations, finding triumph in the past, **NOW.**

# CHAPTER 9

# *Sacred Geometry and The Reptilian Brain*

The Pentagon in Washington, D.C., is the headquarters building of the United States Department of Defense.

A pentagon has five sides and five angles. This type of Pentagon is an irregular platonic solid.

Interior angles measure at 108 degrees -the same distance from the earth to the moon, and mantras are also prescribed as repeating 108 times in reference to this numeracy, as they align to the rhythm of eternity, emptiness, and positivity.

It bridges the ancient world and the modern world, and connects the metaphysical realm to the physical.

This number is significant within sacred mathematics, geometry, astrology, numerology, and in many world religions and spiritual traditions.

In the bible, it is referred to through associations of completeness, divine governance, and cosmic order.

It is said within Indian cosmology that the number 108 is the basis of all creation.

The irony of military-based structure... is it for life, or death?

Each exterior angle measures 72 degrees.

72 is used to determine how to double your investments.

Both measurements add up to 9 at the end of all cycles. Completion, growth: a universally sensitive number... it replicates itself.

War generates money. **(or GOD?) AND TORTURE.**

More and more, it appears as if the US is a drive-thru military base, amongst a gorgeous pastiche of haunted landscapes, of echoed civilizations... and IT HAS a rapt, programmed following.

The military is sold as purity, status, and heroism.

Organized crime comes in disguise.

Or utterly invisible, like a deliberate spectre, that somehow manages to control your movements.

Now, another shape relevant to our discussion here is the **PENTAGRAM.**

A polygon, a five-pointed symbol.

Once a circle is added to its outer points, it becomes a **PENTACLE.**

This is a protective shape inclusive of all directions of the elements, including spirit.

It also evokes Baphomet.

Now, once we pivot this and organize our assemblies to invoke within a geography that shapes this polygon, we resonate and create the power bases to summon forth the work of members and their potent intent.

Such is the workings behind an organized Satanic cult.

Seek – rets So s-high-ety.

If you'll notice, the poles on road lights resemble crosses.

Crossroads.

Leaving offerings to the chosen, at this middle point of directions.

An airplane often resembles this symbol.

Birds in flight. In sects.

Remote views.

There are many operating cults, some linked to certain masters of fortune, and resources... and their allegiances become wildly eccentric, borrowed and overtaken.

Whether it is the Entertainment / Sports Industry, pharmaceutical, medical, tech, data mining, courier, bio tech weaponry, AI, hackers, stalkers, creative scammers, psychic lines...

Privacy is sacred.

There is, or can be, a mafia, gathering, cult, organization, for everything.

There are contingency plans for benefit and survival, if one is willing... the dark web is an illustration of this.

Humanity seeks a curious solvency of the deviant, underground, or dark side.

**The REPTILIAN MIND.**

**THE FAMILIAR?**

Expansive opportunism that allows a certain tier of folks to power, entertain, and replicate the creator or the destroyer, in their finely fuelled quest for more... of **SOMETHING.**

Outside of this, the more sinister side of humanity, exploring dark, unusual fetishes of voyeurism, oppression, and other experimental possibilities, attempts to transmute the synthesis of creatorship, eugenics, as in **THE FALLEN**, hybridization of conscious bombardment and dualism, and the original blueprint of our current amnesiac conditions.

# CHAPTER 10

## *Humiliation and Betrayal Rituals*

My theme seemed to be an unclaimed, simmering power, I had as yet not fully embodied.

I was afraid. I was afraid to own my power. I was afraid to lose love because of it; I never felt I had, and if I claimed my autonomy or substantiated my confidence, regardless of consequences, I would surely die. Alone. And hated.

I forfeited my intuition frequently; still, a daring, necessary independence would separate or alienate me from others.

**MOTHER WOUND.**

Shame and humiliation were not strangers to me.

I barely fit in; I was geeky, defensive, and uncertain as to what to expect from people.

One of the focalizing intentions of being targeted by covens and cults is that you endure rituals that invite and manipulate those around you. **HUMILIATION**

**RITUALS,** designed to knock you down, devastate you, alienate, and isolate you.

The intentions to systematically destroy your life, by attempting to drive you crazy with tech weaponry, burning your brain, your ear cavities, or using some form of black magic, to torture your various bodies, is just not recognized as a fact—**YET.**

**IT CAN AND WILL HAPPEN TO ANYONE IF IT IS NOT ADDRESSED.**

Afraid, AND incensed, I desperately went viral. I valued myself and my life. I was going to save it.

Social media overshares became one such desperate strategy. A humiliating measure of chosen necessity, if I were to survive, and expose this evil.

Reporting, tagging, pleas for help, defiant anger, a cry for justice—this sophisticated, elaborate system of hunting me was far too heady.

Many reports to police, media, and organizations returned little... Transnational reporting requires persistence.

I bombarded them, as a method of coping, and playing back at these psychotic abusers.

Something finally gave; my research on my predators and ample proof led to law enforcement taking these incidents seriously.

But not all, as the whole network was elaborate and included political, judicial, legal bar associations, court systems, and media.

What help I did receive; I was grateful for.

Child exploitation and Trafficking were/is also involved in the folds of these cults.

WHY? Beyond its organized financial reward and high demand, it **RELEASES** an energy.

Folks involved have the means to bribe their way out, and continue the helplessness, stirring joy, they would spectate upon, their victim's torment, and anxiety, yet again, indefinitely.

How dare their innocent victims best them!

And they would meet punishments for it, evoking the rage of what their victims were doing to their reputation, **AND** operation.

To trust anyone in this dilemma becomes a form of uncertain treachery...

Folks so thinly disguised... for a moment.

For some, trust and authenticity **IS** the standard. Others, anything but.

Perhaps it's just too expensive to be one's true self.

If you subscribe to certain services, systems vet you.

If you happen to have an outspoken consciousness raising, or counterculture expression; if you have spiritual abilities, wealth, or if you defy, create envy, or anger the 'wrong' person; the next contestant on 'the Price is Right'...

Meaning... someone is willing to be paid to destroy you, is serious.

# CHAPTER 11

## *Effects of Cult Abuse*

In the book, A Treatise on Cosmic Fire, Alice A. Bailey writes, 'The response of the negative substance concerned, and its moulding into the desired form... pg. 782. Copyright 1962 Lucis Trust

Comprise of

A. The Atomic Substance

B. Molecular Structure

C. Elemental Essence

Further, it states, 'The differentiation is not entirely accurate, and a truer idea of the underlying concept might be conveyed if the word 'energy ' took the place of substance and essence.'

Such a kind distinction, in other words, we are the ultimate wielders of our own form, and the invisible ingredients need only to be recognized, honoured, or fed upon.

After careful study of your details, your birthday, perhaps your birth chart, power numbers associated with **THEIR** associated forces, they begin to intercept their victims by timing that reflects their intention.

If a spell, with a dent of torture, is to start, it will start at 7, or 11... and depending on their own time zones, and what is most expedient for their intentions, they will orchestrate it.

The cult carefully assembles its locations geographically to form a pentagram when it can.

Daily, hourly, by the minute, at times all 200, 300, or 2 of them.

I would see groups, through my psychic ability, of Santerían Priests, attack me in unison, raising my nervous system above and beyond me, to a pulsing and shrill of my senses.

A gangly moment of time stopping, and unbearable pang of just wanting to end this heightened hell, of a stopped minute of sheer nervous, spiritual, and nervous system agony.

A desperate panic would swell to an intolerable level of existence, and anything to relieve it, knowing you are helpless, and caught in such a deep, dark, and overwhelming intention. It certainly tests the boundaries of sanity.

The possibility to end one's life, in those minutes that would stretch out to an eternity, would flicker resistance.

Who could possibly **STOP** this?

**THAT** becomes the helpless horror.

Some are watched and bombarded in the physical realm.

There are targets who have very real, intrusive set ups by gang members, who stalk you, participating in looting your reality, **AND** your safety.

Folks around them contracted to turn against them, follow them, trick them, rob them, evict them, fire them, gaslight, and in essence, betray their safety **ANYWHERE**.

All religions possess sacrificial rites... **FOR EFFECT**, as an **OFFERING**, literally, or metaphorically.

The plan, for the rest of my life, was to literally damage and destroy me.

It is said that we cannot judge where people's evolution lies from lifetime to lifetime. Some have a pleasant, easy life... This may be a preparation for a rigorous karmic journey next, and vice versa.

The common initiations here are the megaliths of **HUMILIATION** and **BETRAYAL**.

These two undoubtedly cause the deepest cuts.

And the potential for the greatest turnarounds in our character.

If we allow.

The purification of pain and near-death experience, that of the ego, but perhaps more, takes us beyond the threshold of the **FAMILIAR.**

...And perhaps the remembered.

What is Voodoo?

According to Wikipedia

Vodun, or vodunsinsen, is an African traditional religion practiced by the Aja, Ewe, and Fon peoples of Benin, Togo, Ghana, Kongo, and Nigeria. Practitioners are commonly called Vodunsentos or Vodunisants.

Vodun teaches the existence of a supreme creator divinity, under whom are lesser spirits called voduns.

Many of these deities are associated with specific areas, but others are venerated widely throughout West Africa; some have been absorbed from other religions, including Christianity and Hinduism. The vodun are believed to physically manifest in shrines, and they are provided with offerings, typically, including animal sacrifices.

There are several male secret societies, including Oro and Egungun, into which individuals receive initiation. Various forms of divination are used to gain information from the vodun, the most prominent of which is Fa, itself governed by a society of initiates.

Amid the Atlantic slave trade of the 16th to the 19th century, vodunsento were among the enslaved Africans transported to the Americas. There, their traditional religions influenced the development of the new religions such as Haitian voodoo, Louisiana Voodoo, and Brazilian Candomble Jeje. Since the 1990s, there have been growing efforts to encourage foreign tourists to visit West Africa and receive initiation into Vodun.

Many Vodoun practitioners practice their traditional religion alongside Christianity, for instance, by interpreting Jesus Christ as a Vodoun. Although primarily found in West Africa, since the late 20th century, the religion has also spread abroad and is practiced by people of varied ethnicities and nationalities.

The deities known as IWA are believed to be present in all aspects of life; their connection is sought through rituals such as drumming, singing, dancing, specific prayers, songs, and veve, spiritual drawings.

The spirits of the LOA are offered to 'accompany' one of the members, receiving communication and guidance.

The IWA are a centralizing component of Haitian Vodou mythology and history, and their stories and traditions are passed down through generations.

The LOA, the major powerful gods of Voodoo, are intermediaries between humans and Bondye, the creator god.

An array of powerful deities with designations to various aspects of both nature, character, and focused intention spectrum, who shall be called upon.

A profound and rich practice of syncretization, empowerment, and mythology.

Voodoo consists of archetypes that were once slaves themselves, as well as an amalgamation of saints and Catholic martyrs.

Offerings include materials such as rum, dolls, cigars, candy, cinnamon buns, and, naturally, this art gets more and more complex and self-created. It is, after all, **AN ART**.

The type of magic, the level of darkness, and the many nuanced things in between make this a very personalized and respected part of culture(s).

Petitions, or rather contracts, are offered to the deities.

These include healing, harming their target, or achieving their desired outcome.

A reverence and call to the deities is enacted by trance, dance, and the permission of the spirit to the body of the devotee.

Usually, there is a request of some kind made of the devotee to fulfil their petitions.

I will now explore the beliefs and practices of Luciferianism, and Satanism, allegedly, prevalent within the deep state, of our governing systems.

Lucifer was known as the 'Light Bringer. He was seen as a guide or guardian, denoting sovereignty, knowledge, self-improvement and deification. He questioned authority and dogma. This symbol of theistic and atheistic tenancy was about the personal will and evolution of human potential.

Satanism, theistic ally worshipped, again, as a rebellious charge against oppressive authority, highlighting freedom, reason, and individualism.

There are different variants of practice, observance and philosophy, fused and lost in sensationalism through Christian interpretations.

The Illuminati, a Bavarian born secret society, made largely of 15 extremely wealthy families, seek world dominance, allegedly as a conspiracy, including over the monarchy, and Christianity.

**New World Order, The Elders of Zion.**

The devil, a symbol of evil, abduction, bargaining of soul, swapping destiny and control, has a wide symbolism - whether Baphonet, Molloch, Saturn, and more.

The use of antisocial, punitive, primal dark emotion and mental elements, with the association of a divinely inspired figure, is where systems and the underworld of human fusion become conducted and corrupt.

The Artes Prohibite, document the black magic systems in all cultures.

The witchcraft hunts and persecutions throughout Europe and the USA in different centuries, so rife with fear and mass murder, was a movement against the fear of natural power, women, the supernatural, but also the ugly unbearable power of the evil will.

We now find a society of paedophilic and dark worship, torture, and theft of humanity, who prize money, control and near dominance.

Unless there is a system which in turn, challenges the paedophile / child / human trafficking movement so ubiquitous; this dark underworld dominance already encroaching on civil liberties and the right to survive reasonably, could be lethal to all.

In the 1990s there were willing individuals with therapeutic and empathic backgrounds willing to create support groups for paedophiles, but we're shut down.

Not all paedophiles are evil.

Most are victims themselves, in proliferation this issue, through generations.

Again... torture, abuse and **THE FALLEN**.

 EACH culture has its own stamp of both positive and negative magic.

Ritual and sacrifice exist everywhere.

The ancient Egyptians would bury some of their denizens, ensuring that the soul continued to be tethered to the continued uses of the living.

In Christian observance, taking of the blood and body of Jesus through wine and wafers, is, somewhat divine necromancy imagined... Christianity of high observance, its tenets are of doing and being 'good', following the divine laws of righteousness, and expressing, and purifying the Most Great High known as God.

Many religions emphasize the desire to evoke and express the best.

# CHAPTER 12
## *Saturn and Cosmic Tools*

The Greek God Cronus, later to be known as Saturn, were associated with time and agriculture. This God was gripped by fear, that his sons would overthrow him. He devoured them to prevent this event. This implying that time devours the ages and gorges —Wikipedia.

The Planet Saturn, a sometimes harsh godfather in a person's chart, has a significant bearing on an individual's development.

In essence, they are overthrown.

A person's Saturn return, which happens every 28 years, (28 days to a menstrual cycle) is a 'transit' that forces a heady maturing process.

One has no choice but to accept losses, cut the frills, and decide what one is best at. It is meant to force one to focus on what they are meant to focus on and achieve.

This is a passage of Mastery, through restriction and discipline.

Saturn is shaped like a hexagon. It has a 6-sided jet stream that encircles Saturn's North pole.

It is comprised of a 6-wave cloud pattern.

Hex means 'witch' in German... hence the famous word for a little bit of unexpected, incidental twizzle.

The hexagram also represents a Hermetic principle of 'As Above, So Below', as well as the union between masculine and feminine.

In Judaism, the six attributes of God are wisdom, majesty, power, love, mercy, and justice.

In Astrological circles, the hexagram is known as 'The King's Star.

The hexagram is a common shape in many religions and cultures around the world.

Eastern, Kabbalistic, and Occult studies.

Christian, and occult thought.

And Arabian magic and witchcraft.

It is a platonic solid.

A 3D shape.

Saturn is the Lord of Time and Karma. He is represented by the black cube. This is the shape of containment and imprisonment.

He is associated with the ruler of this realm, and with the effects, of the Satanic.

In the larger foray of things, it is meant to bind the fallen ones.

It is worshiped by many here.

It is one of the primary images of Metatron's cube, the Archangel Metatron, who is considered God's chosen scribe. Metatron's cube contains the shapes of all existence.

The Christian cross is an unfolded square.

Archangel Metatron is the said architect of this construct. It is a black cube, a platonic solid, which resonates as a star, tetrahedron, and merkaba geometry. The latter is associated with ascension. The blueprint of the system. A pattern that accesses all dimensions, time, and realities.

The cube is a grid, a platonic solid, and contains the structure of reality. It represents the Matrix control, and the parameter of what you shape is real. A fractal infinite structure that replicates itself, trapping cycles, history, and lifetimes.

It is a system that incorporates your body, mind, and energy to be programmed as this geometric pattern. It **BINDS** you to it.

It is found in all religious, mystical, and scientific models of the universe.

It is a soul recycling machine.

This divides and obscures the true original reality of what and who we are.

As VeilBreak states,

The black cube worn on heads, prayed to, and echoed in courtrooms, is a Saturnian Sigil.

Saturn's rings generate sound frequencies used to encode control.

The Saturn—Moon Matrix reflects false light and governs artificial time.

Time, contracts, and limitations are Saturnian constructs -not natural laws.

We live in boxes, and adhere to grids.

As Saturn replaced the sun as the hidden ruler, earth entered a cycle of shadow rulership, with binding contracts masquerading as law, religion, and order.

Chemical, karmic, resonant vibration, frequency, astral, portals, realms, dimensions, some descriptives that defy our gravity, and **3D** myopia.

The hormones regulate and process within the body, akin to reptilian synthesis with the sun, outer planet magnetics, and carry our sacred formulas.

They have a powerful hold on our behaviour, body systems, and attractions.

Our memories are blocked from previous eras, and sacred knowledge from higher levels of our physical, chemical, atomic structures, and DNA can be accessed through our nervous system, pineal glands, and subconscious system.

The many quieter things we go through, almost scientifically or spiritually, couched as whatever makes sense, or grabs hold of our beings, at the most poignant times of our lives, define how we see our connection to this life.

Remember, we come here forgetting.

The womb, in the southern regions, is warm. They are sacred gateways

According to VeilBreak

Modern medicine reclassified birth as a 'medical event' instead of a cosmic passage, disconnecting the soul from ancestry and binding them to maritime law as cargo.

**Birth certificates.**

While death **MAY** be a cold, frightened, kinetic experience, birth IS a hot, messy, temperate adventure, one that one barely remembers.

Death **IS** sublime, and an art in itself.

Death rites were also changed so you would forget real burial customs, stone wrapping, vowel intoning, and northward alignment, so your soul cannot escape this artificial matrix.

The firmament on which we are has hidden many supernormal gateways of locked-away truths that are guarded jealously and vigilantly. The ones who oversee this construct of reality are resourcing their nutrients through our confinement to their victorious temporary clutch, on our planet, our lives, and reality itself.

# CHAPTER 13

## *Highs of Adrenochrome and Plasma*

Certain supermarkets showcase, in their aquariums, bound lobsters... these live beings, still aware of their senses.

Their condition: helpless, curious.

Their pincers tied, as they watch and wonder, their captive status.

Clustered on top of each other, eyeballing, seemingly telepathic, their long feelers gyrating in magnetic instinct.

One could sense they were aware of their capture, divining the heights of suspense, and submitting their wills to a higher process.

I myself, wondered how I had slid through the worst afflictions and affectations to drive me, expel me, to this level of suffering.

The version of my **MOST HIGH** played a major role.

It is speculated that those who are drawn to younger children, as predators, or innocent trauma-echoed partisans, are because they were also annihilated at the same age.

Unless, of course, it is a rite of passage within a cult.

The very prolific demand of babies and children, in circumstances reserved for a certain calibre of being, or allegiance, points to a chemical, a drug-like substance that unleashes a **HIGH**, fed upon by those who have forsaken their sentience, or never had it.

A certain stage of being, containing this chemical, is usually a very young, freshly arrived human baby or a child within the group; it screams trauma, producing this very rare hormone chemical, its adrenals producing the fight or flight secretions.

**SUB STANCES.**

Transgressions the human family entwined within, where women, devastatingly tempting to those angels of **THAT** critical **EPOCH**, the book of **ENOCH** refers to, were wiped from memory. The scapegoated power of the **DIVINE** in women, those **GODS** so taken by the hormonal, electric, magnetic transmissions of these women, wanting desperately to taste the heavenly assignment.

They defied their ultimate master, stealing, seducing and copulating with them; thus, creating **THE GIANTS**, a monstrous result of hybridizing the gods/angels with earthly designation.

Punished by the creator for their insouciance, they were **THRONE** out.

...hence **THE FALLEN.**

Human chemistry changed forever, as well as the league of...

**Chemicals.**

Species from a saltwater ocean copulating with a freshwater DNA, produce... ubiquitous monsters in the sea.

Adrenochrome has been mentioned in connection with the Fallen Stars, their elite status of preserving their youth, and their **EDGE.**

Blood is also a power source of nutrifying plasma, an ancient flow to the DNA carrier of the divine and the fallen.

Both Jesus and **SATAN** revere the blood as an oath and incontrovertible.

**ADRENOCHROME** is the secretion of the adrenal glands, the fight or flight regulators, two sets on each side of our abdomen, near the kidneys. They release adrenaline, said to be a very addictive substance, when regularly ingested.

Adrenochrome is allegedly manufactured by folks who have access to a baby, or child, aborted matter, or blood banks, in order to capture this charged fluid.

Where one donates blood, organs, a rather macabre designation, as well as a life-saving one.

Bloodlines, quality, and memory.

Those, for example, that have been through genocides or holocausts, their agricultural infrastructure decimated, neglected, due to a decision to invest in the universalization of their country, whilst, sacrificing their own citizens... neglecting the upgrade of basic and essential agricultural and survival tools, resulting in humans eating humans; the insanity produced from consuming an already emaciated spirit in high adrenaline, and deficit of mental, and nervous system regulation... is coded into the **DNA** and ancestral lineage, of humankind.

Contemporarily, crops are intentionally destroyed worldwide, the advent of "

'Frankenfood', and the sneaky suspicion, that certain fast food, **IS**... **SOYLENT GREEN.**

**An intake of madness.**

The Ouroboros.

Elixirs of youth.

Whether folks are being cloned on the **BIG** stage, or injected with a cocktail of original sin, the immortal sentience, youthful innocence stolen, is the **HIGH.**

A replication of the original sin. **The FALL.**

Certain folks choose the extenuating evil.

Perhaps they are hardwired for it, chemically or spiritually corrupted as such.

The Bible claims we come here as sinners.

But was it not the **FALLEN** who defied the rules?

Life is boring, to some who cannot affect more for more.

The abuse of power, the desire to explore outside of a unified respect, is perhaps that echo.

With blood magic, cemetery magic, necromancy, etc. there were hidden recipes to soul stealing, skin walking, and such.

Sandra had passed at least 3 times and was revived by this group's effort.

This made the horror of this experience even more agonizing... who would have believed this was possible...

This could go on forever; I would never escape.

She wanted to live so that she could keep doing this endlessly.

She wanted to stay and live longer, stealing energy from anyone—victims, family members, cult members... the theft was very real.

She would endure, to everyone's surprise.

Sandra eventually developed cancer, possibly from the poisonous effects of her evil, the karmic consequences of adrenochrome addiction; plasmic, poisonous, energetic theft.

She eventually ended up in a coma for a year on life support before she passed late 2024.

She had undoubtedly become what is termed a **JINN,** or specific demon, with specific qualities.

Sandra, **THUG**, and Nathaniel had planned to set me up as a human trafficker. They had already devised a strategy. I was also considered to be trafficked. This was to cruelly and sadistically destroy my life.

**THUG** commissioned the destruction of other people within her social circle, as well.

Sandra was charged with child abuse, fraud, and trafficking right after these attempts.

She was incarcerated for 2 months before a very horrible set of circumstances befell her.

She left instructions and funds to continue these operations for life, to myself and other victims.

Nothing is sacred to folks like these, except the evil, to this kind of allegiance.

# CHAPTER 14

## *Reptilian Replication and Alien Tech*

William James would diatribe this stunning thought stream 'There is no doubt that healthy mindedness is inadequate as a philosophical doctrine, because the evil facts which it positively refuses to account for, are genuine portion of reality, and they may after all be the key to life's significance, and possibly the only openers of our eyes, to the deepest levels of the truth'.

My community, once I disclosed my situation in desperation, opened the door to another mass humiliation ritual.

I had no choice but to ask for help publicly, within something so unbelievable, osmotic, and desperately evil, by year 7.

I received all kinds of responses. The desperation of my situation rode over any judgments, disbelief, and criticism.

Some were patently cruel.

Friends of **THUG** could not believe she was capable of what I claimed.

They were wrong.

She had spread lies that I was, in fact, doing harm to others.

A smear campaign and humiliation occurred, in addition to my making this situation public to the media and the police.

She was found guilty, charged, and incarcerated.

As was Sandra's third life partner Manuel Canales.

Previous eras have conveniently erased some of the powerful possibilities our species and epochs have been able to manifest.

Some of these powers coalesce, creating monstrous messes, and are drawn to destroying the purity of innocence, the beauty of transcendence, and shapeshifting, quantum transfer.

There is an equal opportunity, in the duality of things, sourcing the lower levels of dark.

A smoky, intrusive, forbidden spectre of promise, its own layers of hierarchy, and redemptions.

Where some may fear this, or these portals of fright, and unpredictable sensorate, others relish these forms of sinister conduit.

They **ARE** allowed their freedom to practice, but what if their belief systems include the torture of innocent people as necessary, delightful, and absolutely permitted with no remorse or concern?

Luciferians, Satanists, and other choice specialty groups of the Magical arts, Elite, and Corp or ATE culture do not operate exclusively by moral principles, as they are revering selfish, material, and exploitative indulgence.

The Thelemic philosophy is 'do what thou wilt, shall be the whole of the law'.

And if you think you are law unto yourself, perhaps by mental distortion, boredom, and a conditioned sense of sensationalistic intrigue, it likely becomes addictive.

Determined possessed entities want what they want, often with no mercy.

There were over 700 members in **THIS** cult alone.

Today, there are scores of these kinds of controlled opposition factions worldwide.

The signature of their works were distinct.

A partial aspect of this group, their highly organized level of operations, was that they were affiliated with, or funded by, the tier of society that tends to have everything. Clout, money, fraternal allegiance, **POWER.**

What else is there to experience, as immortally rich and conquering connoisseurs of choice?

Greater **HIGHS,** though greater **LOWS.**

Pyrography was an art of culture, whereby beautiful tattoo engravings could be done on bone, with fire.

This art was new to me, and I pondered the spiritual relevance of bones, which hold the memory of cie-al origins, a concentrated memory.

**Hieroglyphs.**

Why do things happen to us...

There is not one answer, through all possibilities of inquiry.

Is it our birth chart... our karma... a lottery of magnetic resonance...

A continuity of scientific or simulated repetition, like a quantum dada ripple?

It is believed some of us endure tests of some order, in some lifetimes, others have it easier; those are resting periods for the ripples of sonic transmission; their cellular functions, winging it, in the world.

Is it just an experience, or a continuation of where we left off before?

Experiencing a slice of our true cosmic radiance in a limited container of expression.

Most of us endure hardships we can't explain away, though we wish to do something about it.

And we can... even if it doesn't matter one day.

An infusion of portals from experimenting with halogen colliders, weaponry, invisible wifis, lowfis, alien military technology that supersedes our sentient barrier, malefic beings hoarding the energy source of our planet, it is for them, either by our emotional struggles, the sonic pitch it creates to beings who function upon hormones or geometric skin that transmutes solar and lunar rays...

Furthermore, **AI LIE N** technology, **AI** is harvested by the collective through WIFI signals.

Our biofields are hacked and diminished.

Telepathy was once our origin within these fields.

We have cell phones, which mimic this capacity instead.

**CHAT GPT** is a portal to interface and invert our own collective memory, like the song of a tribe's original belonging—we are sold back the very unique and original knowledge, already compromised, through a refractive disempowerment.

**Transhumanism.**

Albeit generations born into this technology already sense the frequencies within the womb.

**The REPTILIAN.**

The paedophile.

**The FALLEN...** the result of.

It is also said that light and sound are the beginning of everything... God's voice. His/Her/It's decree, the very first thing ...outside of the darkness and loudness of silence.

All creativity starts with frequency.

The reptilian has a primal gut instinct that embodies a lightning speed of survivalist opportunities, the tongue whips fast, cloven; the ability to progressively camouflage.

How one processes information and senses: attention spans. How is someone stimulated to learn and master?

Not just within a business model...

The hybrid of the nervous system, time travel simulation.

Social media, **DEVI CES,** rewiring and programming synapses... clipped attention through pulsed media, are inducing change to our cognitive fire.

It is a form of syncretism.

Culturally constituted reprogramming of what was once considered a 'normal'

A deliberate shuffle of reality.

Magic doesn't allegedly work, but currency and science do.

Magic, ritual, and machines.

The rays from the brain subtly beam down, every time a thought passes and pauses.

The translations of these rays are what determine the mind's content.

Not the brains.

The mind is not your brain.

It is the precious cargo that arrive **TO** your brain.

Not all these attacks were occult based.

Finely tuned networks all around the world, torture.

Programs developed by the Nazis, instruments created by Tesla and others, later surfaced with mass mind control, expressly in California, the chosen experimental region; executed in events such as the cult disaster of mass suicide, within the Jim Jones phenomenon in the 1960s.

Military grade espionage programs studied the effects of various manipulation tactics.

**COINTEL PRO**, and the similar **MK ULTRA** campaigns, would induce a torture/trauma-based brainwashing and mind control program, spun out, secretly causing forms of repression, persecution, and psychological warfare on its targets.

Some of these were executed by regular people, similar to **STASI Zersetzung Torture.**

There are many companies and organized networks that engage in this kind of activity. Now, in 2025, it is a whopping 8-million-dollar industry, exceeding the educational system budget.

Richard Lighthouse, an author, philosopher, and former engineer at **NASA,** has exposed the systems, that operate these programs, publishing books that assist those who are targeted by these Satanic, counter terrorist groups, who basically label their activities, as a national security measure.

Allegedly, those very people who are able to access information on anyone are behind this activity: the CIA, the FBI, military groups, masonic groups, and elite members of society. They use advanced technology known as DEWS, community groups, and first responders to harass and torture their victims in a multitude of ways.

**Dissidents.**

There **IS**, an alleged lawsuit against Richard Lighthouse, to be a false flag front, who, in fact, is working with the FBI to discredit targeted individuals.

The truth is scary, no matter how you slice it.

Victims' nervous systems are targeted, their bones, the technology can penetrate inside their minds, their inner ears, and their eyes.

Damage is deliberately done to their systems, or they are bombarded with awful suggestions via voice to scull technology.

**I'll say it AGAIN:**

**The power of TORTURE. The archetype of the HERETIC. The PERSECUTED.**

**Timelessness of self is where one pulls from their inner security.**

We are eternal beings, and tapping into this truth, as Jesus himself proclaims, is our 'salvation'.

It is true, those who turn on us know not what they do.

We, in turn, have done it too, somewhere.

There is a well-worn label for certain designs of people; people who exploit without conscience.

They become attached to the charisma and manipulative genius of their persuasive power.

A port of villainous tendency, loyally, over the morality and logic of the event.

Here, jealousy is often rectified.

This type of personality can pull off their own brand of magic and purpose.

The term 'narcissist', has its own functions.

They exercise no limits as to how far they will go, to push an agenda, or intention.

They are the ones who often succeed, the beings looking to preserve a range of 'normality, and hence create progress.

They galvanize a new frontier of progress by virtue of their daring grandiosity.

Is it a new beast, or just more individuals, infected with such conscienceless expression?

It is reminiscent of the Olympics, and the circus, - beings come out bigger than they came in.

The polarity of sensitized people, and those who are interested, or designed to pirate, whatever they can, have become the new divisive quotient in fabricated, resultant culture.

**5G, 5D.**

Opening portals of communication, consideration, and suggestion to systems like ChatGPT is a very metaphorical and literal contract.

Emojis become the contemporary hieroglyphs.

It will become increasingly all too easy and convenient to abdicate our control and consciousness to these systems.

The smearing of what is true and real by **AI lie n** technology threatens, our very traditional conditionings, of what we are originally coming home to.

## BELONGING LOVE ACCOMPLISHMENT HOPE PEACE AND RESOLUTION.

We need to hang on to these, whilst braving new inroads of meaning, in a shuddering drop of technological decisiveness.

The world is going to become a stranger and stranger place, and we must get **FAMILIAR** with it.

# CHAPTER 15

## *Sentience as a Resource*

Sometimes we need to experience humiliation to free ourselves.

The humiliation I found myself stirred by, as I revealed my situation publicly, after many years, became a form of desperate lifesaving, and necessary activism.

At this juncture astrologically, Pluto the underworld transformer, has entered the sign of Aquarius.

Aquarius is about "the group", the **FRATERNAL,** technology, advancements of, and the 'petty ticks' of the masses.

It is also about individuality and the sovereignty of fellow beings.

This influence has the effect of both leader and misfit, designed to futuristically and ingeniously suggest the most rational, and yet, unthinkable concepts.

Uranus, which rules Aquarius, reaches the stratosphere with a flicker of otherworldly prompts, offering a slice of solvency to advance the plight of beautiful humanity, but dreaded mankind.

It is detached emotionally and personally, in order to fine-tune its impressions, that conduit through keen minds; antennae brilliant insights.

The planet Pluto, power broker, ruler of transformation, **SCORPIO**, assigns this planet, the dark underworld destroyer and re-builder of structures.

Again, the sign of humanity, technology, advanced knowledge, **AND THE PEOPLE.**

The activism of these two influences is **PROFOUND.**

'The Keepers of the Dawn' by Barbara Marciniak, in reference to this,

There are beings incarnated here to infuse and anchor other star system energies in order to substantiate certain consciousnesses needed on this planet, beyond the status quo.

Many people are involved in perverse dens of the exploitation of innocence, military advancement, and cooperation with entities. Take that label as you will, that enforce surveilled, monitored, and blinding decrees of free expression, against the sentient "being."

Sentience is a jealously coveted source.

The prevalence of trafficking, snuff, energy, human harvest and cloning, eugenics, and experimental data and mass programming is an attempt to thwart and steal this precious commodity.

The bottom line, pardon my inappropriate pun, but the precious exploitation of innocence, rampant on this planet, is a ubiquitous factor.

Another distilled method to harvest individuals' energies is through the prevalence of sexual abuse, rape, and incest, prevalent to **BOTH** sexes on the planet.

Sexual union and love are a powerful force on this plant, uniting realms into an alchemy of manifestation.

The sacred.

A battery and a frequency.

The reptilian urge aims to confuse the original preference of the child or adult. They are impacted by the act of intrusion, not able to reconcile the **FAMILIAR**, from their true predilection.

A sense of torment is formed and covertness; these conditions of having to pretend, but still be captivated by the echo of abuse, distort their realities, identities, and relationships.

While obviously, **LOVE IS LOVE,** not everyone's conditioning, or identification with what they were traumatized by, is what they cannot easily reconcile.

Innocent sentience is a drug, and more valuable than any other mineral or metal.

There are blood types, lines, and cultural origins that carry a different DNA, or a survivalist one, of which defy the colloquial programming, and maintain, if not magnetize, information and energy, that introduces a higher level of infusion to this **DE VICIVE** and dualistic planet.

It is said that this planet is run by very opportunistic, rough-grade entities that have managed to dupe us into the true capacities of our power.

There are many who will not believe what I am writing, and that is their freedom.

I may be right, I may be wrong, the truth is ever shifting, but it corresponds with a reality that may be hard to capture or access, as we have been compromised to truly integrate it.

We are as the creator, in his\her\its image, **CREATORS vs CREATURES.**

**We are kept creaturely.**

We are, as humans, part of the Kingdom of Mind, as referred to by Alice A Bailey, in her several Christian Buddhist theosophical treatises.

This is exactly what technology is flooding.

Where once our memories were the computer access and recall, the printing press altered... memory was once word of mouth.

**Creatures survive; creators cause.**

Just because someone is desperate does not make them stupid.

Desperation is part of our experience here, and we all variant within this opportunity.

Ultimately, our social circles are also manipulated, programmed, engineered, fabricated, and branded to stay with what seems safest.

Socially, human relief can often come from gossip and association with shared jealousies, insecurities, and projections of superiority. It becomes a basis for belonging, better than someone else.

If someone is destroyed in the process, well, how much more potent the **GANG** becomes.

Gossip can be addictive, as insecurities remain unconquered.

The ability to be brilliantly cruel and reductionist is often rewarded by the group.

This is a venue to shine. Your opinion. Your insecurities.

Pluto in Aquarius and Uranus in Gemini, both high-functioning air signs, thought and speed of light comprehension, the brilliant communicators and curious absorptive ponderers, of **ANYTHING and EVERYTHING.**

One advances the humanitarian stasis, the other bridges heart and mind, expressing inclusion and information synthesis.

How we connect within small talk, designed to associate us, to maintain a harmonious and collective level of relating, within a framework of survival, implies a motion of initiated innocent regard.

We are social creatures, and need each other.

This is the ultimate extortion, when folks are denied belonging.

What you are becomes more important than who you are.

If it reflects well on other power figures in the group, it permits entry.

Respect, conscience, and decorum all have their place.

Your own relationship, to truly treasure, as there are no guarantees anyone else will provide access, loyalty, or frequency to overcome, overstating, and overruling.

The Baghavad Gita states that our relationship to our creator is the most important in our passage here.

# CHAPTER 16

## Media and Cognitive Dissonance

After Sandra passed in 2024, she organized who the reigns of her empire of destruction and the continued trafficking conglomerate would fall upon.

She delegated various people with various duties in the select regions.

They oversaw where and to whom the funds went to continue targeting individuals with torture, harassment, and stalking.

When reports and personal details were handed to law enforcement, even the lack of conscience, the gall to fight for your peace and sovereignty were punished, as they merely wanted to do this unrelentingly until your destruction.

This was, after all, their food.

To steal your energy, peace, and life force.

Highly generated publications that actually SEEMINGLY bravely expose, research, and alert the public, of transgressions to privacy, and unregulated spyware access by **ANYONE**, including corporations, law enforcement, nations at war, and government, were in fact also able to breach, and access the information themselves, and did so.

Media dedicated to informing those interested in how their investment, the investments of large firms that oversee Governments, weaponry, tech genius, and human rights are abused, are **VERY** powerful.

The level of torture on this planet, areas that engage in war, civil targets, dissidents, or insurgencies, is detailed, with deep abiding journalistic and researched alacrity.

A forbidden knowledge, this kind of information compromises the very industries and individuals who import these permissions.

It is almost a cruelty to publish these events, as though they are a cold, hard fact, but unsolvable.

It makes one wonder, how on earth...

Who **IS** truly monitoring human rights?

And who can?

The torturing of global citizens is a steady occupation for those in a position to do so.

Whether it is a political, national, or regional situation, or a domestic interrelationship imprint, it is omnipresent.

It evokes a frequency that releases a certain hormone, a certain frequency that satisfies a primal penchant for a certain design.

The many levels we are blinded to here present this analysis: who is benefiting from this and why?

Is it merely a power surge and flex from those who CAN elicit this kind of condition?

Seemingly sacrificing innocent people or threatening them en masse?

Is it something more sinister?

**MASS SACRIFICE** in a contemporary dissidence?

The frequency of intense fear, terror, and torture, as I mentioned before, releases an energy upon which there are fewer sentient entities who subsist on these expressions, if you will, that feed and harness this outflux of desperate, perhaps, initiated release.

Its signature of pain nourishes their level of survival, and possible domination, or abduction of this realm.

**Are we feeding THE FALLEN?**

Is planet Earth an experiment, a resource, or at times, just a bad, unfair dream?

Our ebullient energies are what we remember, wish to return to, and are our true home.

**Religions and practices are based on it, and, sadly, also abuse it.**

The brokenness of the variance of relations, fairness, and justice, often a credulous mystery, as to how intentions of goodwill for all are wildly unmet.

While there are organizations of benevolence here, dedicated to overseeing the regulation of human and civil rights and freedoms, it scarcely solves the original problem.

Merely a snapshot; a line or two on how perverse and cruel the human condition insists upon itself, in various strata.

Domestic violence, hate crimes, sexual orientation, gender-based violence, and our own psychological inner warfare become an art to navigate.

Those with the luxury of location and perspective can indulge these conditions with a much more progressive address, but many cannot.

When one finds themselves in a situation where no one can stop or help a generated method of torturing, stalking, bullying, and destroying their 'right'? To maintain social course of survival, this becomes a whole new warfare.

**SOME** of the power **BROKE RS** in high stations; oversee this civil rights atrocity.

Many people around the world experience a condition of being targeted in various ways, which cannot always be proven or traced.

They are not believed, and made to look as though they have psychological distortions, by the institutions of such declaration themselves.

The revelry of the **Satanic Ritual Fear, aka SATANIC PANIC,** that raised itself in the 1970s and 1990s, where several accounts of people raised the issue of abuse by this church of philosophy, and its permissive conduct, only to be swept away as a condition of paranoia by the media. Absolutely dismissed. Case closed.

Who was able to completely gaslight a massive cluster of people, as delusional, and why?

During this era, the permissiveness of expanding repressed memory syndrome in psychiatric and psychotherapeutic practices, as a recognized therapy had a motive. In conjunction with abuses, especially sexual abuse, was a ruse to hide the fact that over 12,000 claims of ritualized incidences by everyday citizens, alleged by elites in society, were systematically erased, denied, and rerouted as psychological conditions.

Evidence, police reports, coroners, medical records, legal documents, the list goes on and on—abolished to protect the very insinuations of who was involved.

People are afraid of the daunting truth, and likely more afraid to discover that there is nothing they can do.

The helplessness... is a cultivated state.

It is a consumption.

When someone oversees torture and power, there is a beastly hunger.

We all know hunger needs frequent satiation.

**DISTRACTION, AND ATTRACTION**; the wormhole, within the filler, of this realm, which is provided for you.

It is designed to archetype the consciousness of masses, and individuals, to stream a level of attention, should humanity encounter evolution, as it were, some of the most important energies are present to us, yet we are inexorably diverted. Covert installations of control implemented, confuse, redirect, and steal, a transcending birthright of our genesis.

Who am I to say this is our birthright?

Perhaps this is a realm of hell, and heaven, too.

Everyone is **supposed** to want joy and happiness.

Returning to this feature of this tale, one of the major psychic lines, established in the UK, featured Sandra on the line, even though she had not been actively on the line, as she fell into a year-long coma, and eventually passed.

The company was informed of her activities and serious charges, as well as complaints of her stalking and spiritually harming her callers. In the **USA**, they continued to keep her profile up.

She had been targeting innocent callers, and **STILL,** this did not sway them to fire her.

Though another line in the **USA** did fire her due to others' complaints, this one would not.

This is where I insert my caveat to psychic line users.

It appears, she invested in the **UK** line, and formed a contract to keep her profile up there for public and investigative detours, as well as generating money for the cult activities.

Devin Green, known as **DEMONE** on the line, here in 2025, is following the footsteps of not only chronically abusing the insider's targets, but preying on callers to entertain and feed himself upon the high that is generated from the demonic hatred and greed that takes over these folks.

Why they did not get rid of Sandra, as a protective upstanding and ethical business of this sort 'would', it is another venue as a trafficking ring, including hotels and tech companies, extending themselves from the UK, to South America.

Manuel Canales, her 3rd partner, oversaw conglomerate involvements, investments, and organizations of all sorts overseas.

He was connected to the tech side of torture, enabling microwave and DEW weaponry to target organs, glands, etc.

Many a morning, I had woken up with numb hands and lasers targeting my hypothalamus and pituitary glands.

The pain was so intense that I imagine it was to elicit a stroke; I vomited from the sheer intensity of it.

It would last for hours.

Even EMF copper wraps could scarcely block the intense pulsation and precision of the aim.

I knew it was Manuel's methods, as they stopped once he was incarcerated.

Charges and prison sentences that do not stretch long enough see these transgressors coming out, only to resume their practices on new and old targets.

# CHAPTER 17
## *Multi-Dimensional Heritage*

Law enforcement becomes overwhelmed by how to handle these transnational issues, delegating certain felonies to departments, which minutia becomes stalled, without the larger picture of evidence, and confessions spilled.

As we are prompted, literally, to merge with **AI Lie N** technology, and its ability to recreate our realities, obscuring what is real and true, a treachery? Of obliterating our organic functions and perceptions, a technology capable of inducing a whole new abstract, on its own self-regulating finite of data replication and evolution, we can barely control or trace, where this infinite application will render us, is indeed an annihilating fear.

A crude replication, a simulation of the **CREATOR** itself.

Perhaps, it is meant this way, in this realm. A temporary drive-by shooting of our moments here, how many species have come and gone according to our documents.

We, too, may be temporary creatures with a different karma to fill.

This synthetic introduction part of the schema.

Perhaps we need to be impersonal about our limited time here; this realm has its functions, and as Gary Renard from his book 'The Disappearance of the Universe' suggests, it is all a dream, a separation from the creator dreamt by humankind, that moment of condensed time we experience in a very slow 3d dumbness, where time is a construct of compressing our ability to transgress, forgiveness of everything, as the ultimate persecuted master, Christ of the light, the sun, the bright birth of revelation and ascension, imparts to us.

A mystical state of understanding, they know not what they do.

This place ain't fair.

That is perhaps not its purpose.

This is why gossip and news are a relief.

It mimics a covert justice.

The unification of the collective is in harmony with a select compartment of filler.

Music, art, sports, activism, performance, mastery, religion, spirituality, and organization set most of us free.

The invisible world.

Freedom looks different in different stages of our lives, even when we cease, this mortal coil.

Whether it is the wisdom of a birth or death doula, it is the poignant **MOMENTS** we ultimately treasure as our most important accomplishments.

**The Rolling Stones sing in their 'It Won't Take Long' track, off 'The Bigger Bang' album, 2005: 'All I have is a shoe box of Memories'.**

**THE FAMILIAR.**

To get inside the minds of folks who thrive on destroying others is unfathomable to many; yet, it is exercised by many.

Does religion fix this? Does art? Does money?

We know the answer.

The roots and minerals of the earth have been mined as a resource for the currency of our transactional debt to arrive here.

Born fallen and in debt, salvation is transcendence.

That is the equation.

Our phantom multidimensional heritage is crippling to many who are sensitive, remember, or struggle to return to this natural and original 'state'.

Those who struggle with depression and other psychological factors, talented, sensitive, or complicated by spiritual cross currents, are barely given merit, exemplifying the condition of cloistered range.

The transformation of lead (Saturn) into gold (the sun). Alchemists tinkered with capturing the secret of life, the philosopher's stone, embodying science, mathematics, quantum escape, and immortal encapsulation.

These types of experiments were funded, of course, by orthodox intention; as the technologies designed to steal / preserve secrets, freedoms, and sentience of life are now.

Inventors who were able to solve some of the environmental issues were shot down in the early stages of 90s environmentalism.

There are folks out there who purchase patents in order to keep them from being created, to spare their destructive uses.

See Tesla and his invention of the death ray for the government.

His error was in being a peacock.

Also, utterly used, abused, and destroyed by those parties seeking his genius patents.

The phenomenon of Targeted Individuals, or **TIs** as they are called, is becoming more and more ubiquitous.

The striking element about this is that none of them receives help.

There are many, many people involved with these activities, **WORLDWIDE.**

Persecution has long been perpetrated, typically by a criminal permission.

The Salem witch trials, which also theatrically drove the natural wisdom of women, and those connected to ancient knowledge, were brutally destroyed, ushering in a patriarchal, medical, political, and religious hierarchy.

Most nations eliminate their native populations, who are typically mystical warriors, who have their own ancestral codes of DNA distinction.

The North American Natives dealt with transgressions in an equitable and compassionate manner.

Those who transgressed within the community were brought around a circle within the collective, and empathically interrogated, with the aim to bring awareness and a breakthrough upon their behavioural choices.

Often it was a ritual of healing not only the offender, but the tribe.

The barbarism of our species is indeed a sad truth.

We are all mesmerized by our reality, whether we know it or not.

When the very part of our society is being annihilated by the very paternal protectorships, are the very people themselves enacting these cruel hunting games of a section of society...

Torture is indeed a weapon of the sadistic.

The Entertainment Industry, the Sports Industrial complex, are very powerful means to control, ritualize, and siphon the mass energy of a population.

To be on the wrong side of things... without trying.

Here it begs a diplomacy about God.

IS the creator personal? Or consequential?

The one big saviour was also persecuted...

Why?

Why is there such fear for a species' autonomy?

Many victims share that they have only become stronger through their faith, their spiritual legacies, and alignments.

Even when those all around them betray them.

The intention again is to isolate and destroy these people's abilities to thrive, love, feel joy, magic, prosper, evolve, heal, be blessed, and make a difference, big or small.

The status of becoming aligned with professions requires an allegiance to the academy as such.

Much like a secret society, and some religious / spiritual institutions / cults.

Who saves us from corruption?

There is a grief to traverse, as our lives are abducted, and sabotaged at almost every turn, by an organized group of people, funded by **SOMEWHERE** in droves globally, and again, no one can, or **WILL** help. So far, no one cares, much less knows what to do for the targeted.

The level of proof for each victim is outstanding.

**NO ONE LISTENS.**

Well... yes, they do.

And watch.

A hunted voyeurism.

# CHAPTER 18

# *Addiction and The Super Ordinary*

Self-love is one of the strongest anathemas to such activity. No one can take you away from yourself.

This **IS** the cross to bear.

Will there be breakdowns and utter helplessness?

Oh yes.

When one finds themselves at a crossroads, presented with folks who don't know you, or care to, but see you as an offering to their altars...

The timelessness of our beings is a key; at some point, we have done everything, and remembering a 'time' when we were able to offset this powerfully is a reach for those in need of it.

Indeed, torture is a powerful food source for a certain faction of forces that seem to be multiplying and conducting our genesis.

**The ART OF THE MOMENT** is all there is, once you screw your mind to the battle.

It mimics peace, as it were, bravery. Defiance. Defence.

**Mi Lit ary.**

Archetypes and Avatars range from function and purpose.

It is no mistake that video games simulate the supernatural.

The spiritual battles are **FAMILIAR.**

As there are bloodlines and lineages, some come from the line of The Heretic and the lineage of Persecution.

Speculative origins of Humankind... the architects of reality... some of which are **THE FALLEN** angels.

These are the holders of secrets, the forbidden knowledge since TIME'S inception.

The Nephilim, or **AI LIE Ns**, were the Gods of old, shaping the ancient world, and erasing it from memory.

The timelines of our history have been shifted and altered, rendering us with the amnesia we are cognitively dissonantly induced.

Some of these 'Angels' betrayed their purpose and chose instead to battle both time and space. Their genesis is scattered across cultures.

It is possible that the Great Flood was meant to eliminate the offspring of the fallen—the Nephilim.

Angels are both gentle and loving, as they are ferocious.

There are alleged leagues of them.

Interdimensional beings that oversee the cosmic bending of dimensions.

They hold a stance of battle in the quiet scheme, still unfolding.

Tribes of the Dan, the Scythians, and Israel migrated north, connected to this ancient knowledge.

They are the Formulators of European Secret Societies, who still control the world in a highly sophisticated organization.

The black cube of Saturn, Lord of Time and Karma, interfaces with the imprisonment and the binding of the Fallen.

They were cast beneath the earth, sealed until judgment.

Secret Societies may well be the workers who are looking to free their Masters.

**CERN,** in Switzerland, accelerates particles in an attempt to break the veils of the angelic dimensions that threaten to separate our dimension of imprisonment.

**NASA** confirms a parallel universe through Antarctica, a prison breaking apart, the battle for power and reality.

**AI LIE N.**

AI and multiverse replication.

Heaven and Hell are parallel universes.

David Bowie, in his tome, **BLACK STAR**, circa 2016, sings of being 'born upside down, born the wrong way round'.

As a dying visionary, able to peer into the void of death, he declared, in his song I can't **GIVE** everything **AWAY**.

The idea of a jealous God, due to Original Sin, equals Original Revenge—The Fall.

The God's mistakes are our punishment.

We are the downgraded chattel of the battle.

We are made in God's image.

This is our true connection and inheritance.

The Constellation of the Anus is, in fact, a portal.

It **IS** shaped like a star.

The ears and sacred opening of a woman, the ocean... dynastic infinity.

The lingam, a fleshy cord to the fire of inner earth and sea, the weight of a feather in height.

The intestines simulate black holes.

**The H EAR T... HEAVEN, and Middle-earth, to the other side.**

As a compensation for a missing piece of our memories, many of us turn to distraction and addiction to escape the mysterious dullness of our haunted amnesia.

It also attempts to simulate a connection to the phantom high we once existed within.

It is a bit more involved, with interdimensional obscuration.

Our connection to the elements, and the chosen methods of escape, or inspiration, emulating connection with the higher, or in some cases, the lower.

Our communities, and our place in them.

The realm of water and liquid parallels the spirits of alcohol. Smoke with fire **THE DRAG ON,** vapour the invisible or etheric, poking the streamline of interdimensional waking, snorting the defiant heir of the sensitive mind, the roots of gambling, which also plays with the high of chance, sex, the root of power and procreation, the orgasmic breath and sensation of life and electrical conduction... or you can **SCROLL** your life away, on the **DEAD SEE SCROLLS.** All these are scattered in pleasure, and those that take it away, pain.

The sensation of a shooting star.

**The Search for Glory.**

The psychology behind torture, inspired by sadism, the annihilation of one's peace and liberty, in a helpless inducing a high.

We are at a time where the Divine Feminine is regenerating her stolen power.

The Divine Masculine is wounded by programmed confines.

The siphoning of Divine energy is the goal of these parasitic systems and beings.

It is also the sublime, where many answers are discovered.

These experiences often lead the victim to a high state of surrender of their spirituality and their core convictions, beyond time and space.

Ritual often ingredients sacrifice.

It is a **FAMILIAR...**

And freedom is either the separation of what's **FAMILIAR, or straight to it.**

**We may need an uprising of Counterintuitive Exposure and Dominance.**

# CHAPTER 19
## *The MA SONS*

Fortifiers of the 'temple' stone.

Tombstones a metaphor of this mastery.

A monopolized and regulated institution of burial, art, sacred restoration of temples, and the preservation of exclusivity; the secrets of ancient knowledge.

Our sentience and energy are sacred to us.

Death is as much of an art as is life.

**LOVER, OF GREAT MOMENTS:**

**FILL**

**YOUR**

**SHOO BOX.**